Pierre Carlet de Marivaux

THE SUPRISE OF LOVE

La Seconde Surprise de l'Amour

Translated by Mike Alfreds

T0347798

OBERON BOOKS
LONDON

WWW.OBERONBOOKS.COM

Characters

THE MARQUISE
a widow

LISETTE
her maid

LUBIN
the Chevalier's valet

HORTENSIUS
a scholar

THE CHEVALIER

THE COUNT

Paris, 1727.

This translation of *The Surprise of Love* was commissioned by Theatre Royal Bath, and was first performed in the Ustinov Studio, Theatre Royal Bath on 9th November 2011 with the following cast:

THE MARQUISE Laura Rees

LISETTE Frances McNamee

LUBIN Peter Bramhill

HORTENSIUS Christopher Hunter

THE CHEVALIER Milo Twomey

THE COUNT Adam Jackson-Smith

Director, Laurence Boswell

Designer, Ti Green

Co-Lighting Designers, Ben Ormerod and Richard Howell

Sound Designer, Fergus O'Hare

Movement Director, Jonathan Howell

SCENE 1

The MARQUISE enters sadly, unaware that LISETTE is following her.

MARQUISE: *(Coming to a halt with a sigh.)* Ah!

LISETTE: *(Behind her.)* Ah!

MARQUISE: What's that? Ha! it's you?

LISETTE: Yes, Madame.

MARQUISE: What have you got to sigh about?

LISETTE: Me? Nothing: You sighed, I took that for an attempt at conversation so I sighed back.

MARQUISE: Oh, indeed; and who told you to follow me?

LISETTE: Who? You called me, so I came; you wandered off, so I followed; now I'm waiting.

MARQUISE: I did? I called you?

LISETTE: Yes, Madame.

MARQUISE: Off with you, you've been dreaming, back the way you came; I don't need you.

LISETTE: Back the way you came! Grief-stricken people shouldn't be left alone.

MARQUISE: This is no concern of yours; leave me be.

LISETTE: It only increases the grief.

MARQUISE: I find my grief gratifying.

LISETTE: And it's for those who love you to help you out of your grief; I shan't be the one to let you die of despair.

MARQUISE: I'd like to see how you go about that!

LISETTE: Dear heaven! We're supposed to use some common sense in life, which means not picking fights with people who care about us.

MARQUISE: I have to say, your efforts are most effective: trying to take me out of my torment, you've managed to put me in a temper.

LISETTE: At least it's a distraction; better to quarrel than sigh.

MARQUISE: Ah! leave me alone, I owe his memory a lifetime of sighs.

LISETTE: Did you say 'Owe him'! Oh! that's a debt you'll never pay; you're far too young to start making vows for life.

MARQUISE: What I said is true, true: there's no longer any consolation for me, ever; after two years of the most tender courtship, to marry the man you love, the most lovable person in the world, to marry him, and after a month to lose him!

LISETTE: A month! At least you've salvaged something. I know a woman who had her husband for just two days; now that really hurts.

MARQUISE: I've lost everything, I tell you.

LISETTE: Everything! You make me tremble: is every other man in the world dead?

MARQUISE: Eh! what do I care about other men?

LISETTE: Ah! Madame, listen to yourself! Heaven protect them! You should never turn up your nose at what's available to you.

MARQUISE: Available! To me, when all I want is to bury myself in my grief! To me, when I'm alive only by an effort of will!

LISETTE: What d'you mean by an effort of will? I don't believe that for a minute! For someone who's pining away, you look remarkably fresh.

MARQUISE: Lisette, I beg of you, no more jokes; you can be very amusing at times, but this isn't one of them, I'm not in the mood.

LISETTE: Ah, come, Madame, seriously, you're looking more radiant than ever; look at it like this: when life was good to you, you weren't perhaps quite so beautiful; now life's treating you badly, you look so much livelier, your eyes are sparkling, they're rebellious, I suggest you keep up your battle against life; that will do you more good than you can imagine.

MARQUISE: You're mad! I didn't close my eyes all night.

LISETTE: Maybe you fell asleep and dreamt you couldn't sleep? If your complexion is anything to go by, you look wonderfully rested, a little tousled maybe. I'm of the opinion that your *coiffure* deserves a slight readjustment. *(Calls off.)* La Brie, bring Madame her dressing table.

MARQUISE: What are you up to? I don't want it.

LISETTE: You don't want it! You refuse your mirror, a mirror, Madame! D'you realise how much you're frightening me! Let's be serious and deal with this once and for all: I am not going to tell you how charming you are without some positive action on your part: I insist you look and see for yourself, it'll make you feel so much better, you'll recapture your pleasure in living. *(The dressing table is brought in; she takes hold of a chair.)* Now, Madame, put yourself here, so I can tidy you up: believe me, that Doctor of Philosophy you've brought into the house will never read you anything half as consoling as what you're about to see in your mirror.

MARQUISE: Oh! you're driving me mad: why do I need to look better than I actually feel? I'm not planning to see anyone.

LISETTE: For mercy's sake, a quick glimpse in the mirror, a tiny peek; a sideways glance, give it a try.

MARQUISE: If only you'd leave me in peace.

LISETTE: Amazing! You've abandoned all self-respect and you're still breathing – that's not natural. You're deluding yourself. Must I speak frankly? I told you you're more beautiful than ever; but the truth is you've changed a lot, too; I wish you'd take some pity on your

	appearance, you've been neglecting yourself brutally.
MARQUISE:	What is the point, my situation is hopeless.
LISETTE:	Then there's nothing for it but to remove your dressing table? La Brie, take it back where you found it.
MARQUISE:	Accomplishments, appearance, they no longer concern me in the slightest.
LISETTE:	Did you hear? Your mirror's about to be removed.
MARQUISE:	But, Lisette, do I actually look so dreadful?
LISETTE:	Extremely changed.
MARQUISE:	Then I'd better take a look, I suppose, if that's the way to get rid of you.
LISETTE:	Ah! I breathe again, you're saved. Now, Madame, be brave! *(The mirror is brought back.)*
MARQUISE:	Hand it to me, you're right, I'm utterly worn down.
LISETTE:	*(Handing her the mirror.)* Wouldn't it be a crime to let this complexion fade, it's nothing but lilies and roses when it's cared for? Let me arrange your hair, it's all over the place and it's hiding that fire in your eyes: ah! those devils, were they aimed at me, I'd be burnt to a crisp; they're just looking for trouble.
MARQUISE:	*(Returning the mirror.)* You're imagining things; they're dying embers.
LISETTE:	Dying embers indeed. They're just lying in ambush: dare the enemy advance, they'll burst into flame! Look, here comes one of the Chevalier's servants, his valet, I think, that funny country lad that made you laugh a while back.
MARQUISE:	What does his master want with me? I'm not receiving callers.
LISETTE:	We ought to find out.

SCENE 2

LUBIN, MARQUISE, LISETTE

LUBIN: Madame, forgive the disturbance…

LISETTE: Get to the point; you seem to think you're
               entitled to disturb Madame.

LUBIN: And you seem to think you're entitled to
               interrupt me, darling. Aren't I allowed to
               conduct myself in a decent manner?

MARQUISE: Enough, what brings you here?

LUBIN: What brings me here, Madame, are Monsieur
               the Chevalier's instructions to…what your
               maid's made me forget.

LISETTE: What a crank!

LUBIN: That's true; but when I'm upset, I forget.

MARQUISE: Then go back and find out what you're here
               for.

LUBIN: Oh! not necessary, Madame, I've just
               remembered; it's that we arrived back in
               Paris yesterday, Monsieur the Chevalier and
               myself, and we're going away tomorrow and
               never coming back; which is why Monsieur
               the Chevalier sends word that you will find
               it acceptable if he doesn't see you after
               dinner, since he can only pay his respects this
               morning, if that doesn't displease you, to bid
               you adieu, because of the inconvenience of
               his arrangements.

LISETTE: All this gibberish means that Monsieur the
               Chevalier wishes to see you right now…

MARQUISE: Do you know what he wants with me? I am in
               very unhappy circumstances.

LUBIN: *(Sadly and ending in tears.)* He wishes to ask if
               you will have the goodness to give him fifteen
               minutes conversation; as for unhappiness,
               don't be concerned, Madame, he won't
               interfere with yours; he's got more than

	enough of his own, me, too; everyone feels very sorry for us.
LISETTE:	Don't tell me he's crying.
LUBIN:	Oh! this is nothing, I cry very differently when I'm alone; but now I'm restraining myself out of consideration.
LISETTE:	Stop that noise.
MARQUISE:	Tell your master I'm expecting him; and you, Lisette, the moment Monsieur Hortensius gets back, make sure he shows me the books he bought for me. *(She sighs as she leaves.)*

SCENE 3

LUBIN, LISETTE

LISETTE:	There she goes, sighing again, and you're the cause, you lout; we've had enough trouble from your tears.
LUBIN:	Take 'em or leave 'em. They seem to have gone down well with Madame, and Monsieur the Chevalier will be even more to her taste, he sighs even better than I do.
LISETTE:	He can keep his sighs to himself; tell him not to let her see how unhappy he is. That's why I tried to stop you; my mistress already has more than her fair share of misery and I'm trying hard to shake her out of it: d'you understand?
LUBIN:	Heavens! You don't have to shout.
LISETTE:	And you don't have to be rude. So! are we allowed to know what the two of you are crying and sighing about?
LUBIN:	Nothing, really: myself, I cry when I want to, if I wanted, I could be a laugh a minute.
LISETTE:	Oh! a joker.
LUBIN:	Yes, my master sighs because he's lost his mistress, as for me, I've got the most

	sympathetic heart in the world, so I cry along with him just to cheer him up.
LISETTE:	*(Laughing.)* Ah, ah, ah, ah!
LUBIN:	*(Laughing.)* Eh, eh, eh! you're laughing about it, I laugh about it sometimes, too, but not too often, as it upsets me. I've also lost a mistress, myself, but since I'll never see her again, I'll still love her but without feeling sad about it. *(He laughs.)* Eh, eh, eh!
LISETTE:	Quite the entertainer. Now off you go: give your master his message, and make sure you warn him of what I said.
LUBIN:	*(Laughing.)* Off I go, off I go.
LISETTE:	What's this then, it looks as if you're eyeing me up?
LUBIN:	There's no if, I am eyeing you up.
LISETTE:	That'll cramp your style if you plan to do any more crying.
LUBIN:	D'you want to bet... Shall I show you?
LISETTE:	Go away; your master's waiting.
LUBIN:	I'm not the one holding things up.
LISETTE:	I'm not getting involved with a man who's going away tomorrow: take yourself off.
LUBIN:	You're right about that, it's not worth any more discussion. So farewell then, my girl.
LISETTE:	Good morning, my boy.

SCENE 4

LISETTE alone

| LISETTE: | That clown's amusing. But here comes Monsieur Hortensius, loaded like a bookshelf. He's boring us all rigid with his stupid learning! Heaven only knows what got into my mistress's head, making this 'personage' part of the household, to direct her reading |

and distract her in her grief! What bees these 'ladies' do get in their bonnets!

SCENE 5

HORTENSIUS, LISETTE

LISETTE: Monsieur Hortensius, Madame's instructed me to remind you to show her the books you've just purchased.

HORTENSIUS: I shall be punctual to obey, Mad'moiselle Lisette; and Madame the Marquise gave her instructions to a person who makes them even worthier of my prompt obedience.

LISETTE: Ah! What a lovely turn of phrase! Really! You greet me with the most flattering arrangement of words possible, and I can tell it issues from the lips of a man who knows his rhetoric.

HORTENSIUS: Any rhetoric I know on that subject, Mad'moiselle, is what your beautiful eyes have taught me.

LISETTE: You astonish me; I had no idea my beautiful eyes were professors of rhetoric.

HORTENSIUS: They've inspired my heart to compose a thesis, Mad'moiselle; and, as a sample of my science, I shall, if it's agreeable to you, give you a brief argument in appropriate form.

LISETTE: An argument for me! I don't know about that; I'd rather not sample the sample. I really should go.

HORTENSIUS: Wait, listen to my little syllogism; I promise you the logic is inescapable.

LISETTE: A syllogism! Eh! what do you want me to do with one of those?

HORTENSIUS: Listen: One's heart belongs to those who give you theirs; I have given you my heart: *ergo*, you owe me yours.

LISETTE:	Is that it? Oh! I can do rhetoric too. Listen: One's heart belongs to those who capture it; you certainly haven't captured mine: *ergo*, you won't get it. Good day.
HORTENSIUS:	*(Stopping her.)* Reason replies…
LISETTE:	Oh! as for reason, I don't ever get mixed up in that, girls my age don't have any dealings with reason. Goodbye, Monsieur Hortensius; may heaven smile on you, your thesis and your syllogisms.
HORTENSIUS:	But I've composed some short Latin verses on your charms.
LISETTE:	Oh but, Monsieur Hortensius, my charms only understand French.
HORTENSIUS:	One could translate them for you.
LISETTE:	Not now, I must be off.
HORTENSIUS:	I think I tucked them inside a book somewhere…
LISETTE:	*(While he burrows about for them, she sees the MARQUISE approaching.)* He can look for his papers with the mistress. *(She leaves.)*
HORTENSIUS:	*(Continuing to shuffle through his books.)* I have named you Helen, in the most poetic of forms, and I've taken the liberty of calling myself Paris of the legend: here they are, most elegant.

SCENE 6

HORTENSIUS, MARQUISE

MARQUISE:	What are you talking about, calling yourself the legendary Paris, who are you talking to? Show me the paper.
HORTENSIUS:	It's a treatise on Greek history, Madame, about which Mad'moiselle Lisette asked for some elucidation.

MARQUISE:	She's very enquiring, and you're very obliging; where are the books you bought me, Monsieur?
HORTENSIUS:	I have them with me, Madame, all in excellent condition and at a very reasonable price. Do you wish to see them?
MARQUISE:	Show me.
LA BRIE:	*(Entering.)* Monsieur the Chevalier is here, Madame.
MARQUISE:	Show him in. *(To HORTENSIUS.)* Take them to my study, we'll look at them later.

SCENE 7

CHEVALIER. MARQUISE.

CHEVALIER:	Forgive what must be an intrusion, Madame; especially when I know what you're going through.
MARQUISE:	Ah! not in the least, it's a pleasure: can I be of some service: what brings you here? You seem so unhappy.
CHEVALIER:	Madame, you're looking at a man in despair, about to bury himself in his birthplace, in the far depths of the country, there to live out a life that's become a burden to him.
MARQUISE:	What are you saying? You alarm me; what has happened?
CHEVALIER:	The worst disaster imaginable, the most agonising…irreparable: I have lost Angélique; and I've lost her forever.
MARQUISE:	How? Don't tell me she's dead?
CHEVALIER:	As good as, to me. Eight months ago she went on a retreat, you remember, to escape the marriage her father was forcing on her; we both hoped that this would soften his resolve; he kept up the pressure; and she, apparently ground down by his relentless bullying,

accustomed by now to my absence from her side and, no doubt, losing hope of ever seeing me there again, gave up the struggle, gave up the world, retreated from it completely and has bound herself with vows she can never break. This was two months ago. I saw her on her last day of freedom, pleaded with her, laid my despair before her, but my desolation, my prayers, my love: all useless. I was left to be the witness of my own misfortune; ever since I've been staying in her neighbourhood, I had to force myself away, I only got back yesterday. I'm dying, I want to die, and why I'm still alive I don't understand.

MARQUISE: Indeed, it seems that in this world sufferings are always visited on the decent people.

CHEVALIER: I should have kept my suffering to myself, Madame, you're only too afflicted with your own.

MARQUISE: No, Chevalier, say what you feel, your grief speaks in your favour; to me, it's a virtue; I'm inspired by such depth of feeling; nowadays, alas, it's so rare! there's no longer any refinement, consideration; myself, here, talking to you, people find it incomprehensible that after six months I can still be weeping; they'll take you for an oddity, too; I'll be the only one truly capable of sympathising with you, and you'll be the only one with the ability to respect my tears, we're so alike: you were born with so much sensitivity, I really see that.

CHEVALIER: It's true, Madame, my grief doesn't prevent my being moved by yours.

MARQUISE: You don't need to convince me of that. But your visit: how can I help you?

CHEVALIER: I'll never see Angélique again; she has forbidden it and I wish to obey her.

15

MARQUISE: That's just the way a decent man should think.

CHEVALIER: This letter – I've no way of delivering it, she won't receive it from me. You often visit your country place, it's near where she now lives; do me the favour, I beg of you, give it to her yourself; the only indulgence I ask of her is to read it; and if I in turn can ever do something for you, Madame...

MARQUISE: *(Interrupting.)* But who could refuse you – endowed with true tenderness, compassionate from birth – it goes without saying; I now know your character like my own; good-hearted people are alike, Chevalier: but the letter's not sealed.

CHEVALIER: I don't know what I'm doing, the distress I'm in. Since it's open, you read it, Madame, you'll judge better what sympathy I merit; then we can talk further and at length; something tells me that whatever you have to say to me will be of comfort.

MARQUISE: Believe me, without a word of flattery, this is the first moment in six months I've found bearable; and why? Because it's a relief to grieve freely in the company of someone who understands. But the letter. *(Reading.)* 'I had intended to see you again, Angélique, but realising how much I'd be going against your wishes, I restrained myself. After all, what would I have achieved? I barely know what I'd have said; all I do know is that I've lost you, that by talking to you I was seeking to redouble the agony of that loss, until it penetrated my whole being to the point of death.' *(She interrupts her reading to repeat the last words.)* 'Until it penetrated my whole being to the point of death.' But that's astonishing: what you write here, Chevalier, is what I've thought word for word in my own agony; is it possible to be in such harmony! In truth, my feelings are stirred by such respect for you! Let's finish the letter. *(She continues reading.)* 'But it's over, and I'm writing only to beg your forgiveness for what escaped my lips at out last meeting. You were leaving me forever, Angélique, I was desperate; and in that moment, I loved you far too much to be fair to you; my reproaches cost you tears, I chose not to see them, I chose only to see you as the guilty one, and for you to admit it; in doing so I offended against Virtue itself. Adieu, Angélique, my love for you will only die with my death, and I renounce all possible future commitments. My sole wish is that you find these last expressions from my heart of sufficient worth to justify the love you honoured me with.' *(She hands back the letter.)* Well, Chevalier, a man who reveals such feelings is in no need of sympathy; what a letter! My husband once wrote something similar to me, I thought him the only man in the world capable of such delicacy; you were his friend, so it shouldn't surprise me.

CHEVALIER: You know how precious his friendship was for me.

MARQUISE: He only bestowed it on those who deserved it.

CHEVALIER: What a great comfort it would be, if he were still alive!

MARQUISE: *(Weeping.)* In that, we've both lost him…

CHEVALIER: I don't believe I'll outlive him long.

MARQUISE: No, Chevalier, live and allow me the comfort of mourning him with his friend; and in place of his friendship, I offer mine.

CHEVALIER: What more could I ask of you, your friendship will be my sustenance; I'll take the liberty of writing to you, surely you'll reply, and that's the comforting hope I'll carry away with me.

MARQUISE: To be honest, Chevalier, I wish you were staying; with you alone I seem able to give free rein to my unhappiness.

CHEVALIER: If I did stay, I'd break with the rest of the world, you'd be the only one I'd wish to see.

MARQUISE: But in effect, what good will going away do you? Ask yourself: and I'm sure you'd feel more at peace not quite so far from Angélique.

CHEVALIER: True, and at times I could talk of her with you.

MARQUISE: Yes: at least I'd be here to offer sympathy, and you could offer sympathy to me; that way, the pain would be more bearable.

CHEVALIER: Really and truly, I do believe you're right.

MARQUISE: We are neighbours.

CHEVALIER: It's almost as if we lived in the same house, we share a common garden.

MARQUISE: We're both grieving, we think alike.

CHEVALIER: Friendship will be our consolation.

MARQUISE: Then you do agree: this is the sole resource we have in our affliction. Do you care for readings?

CHEVALIER: Very much.

MARQUISE: Even better; two weeks ago, I took on a scholar to organise my library; I have no academic pretensions myself, but it passes the time pleasantly enough: every evening he reads me something, the selections are serious, thoughtful; he's arranged them to be instructive as well as diverting: would you care to be one of the party?

CHEVALIER: It's done, Madame, you've made up my mind for me; it's my good fortune I came to call on you; I feel calmer already. It's decided then,

I shan't be going away: I've quite a large number of books myself, this man you've hired to care for yours can arrange both lots together; I must call my valet and change his orders. How much I owe you! You may have saved my sanity, my despair is lifting. You have a gentleness of disposition that's exactly what I needed, it's taken possession of me. You've renounced love, I, too; your friendship will replace everything – if you're susceptible to mine.

MARQUISE: In all seriousness, I feel that I have an obligation, almost, to compensate you for the loss of my husband's friendship: go, Chevalier, make your arrangements quickly; I've also things to do; we'll meet again soon. *(Aside.)* In all honesty, this man's integrity soothes my sorrows.

SCENE 8

CHEVALIER

CHEVALIER: *(Alone for a moment.)* These truly are the proper sentiments to console a person in despair; what qualities this woman possesses! I never really knew her before; what strength of spirit! What goodness of heart! Her character is a little like Angélique's, such characters as theirs are to be treasured; yes, I place her above all the friends in the world. *(He calls.)* Lubin! That's him, I think, in the garden.

SCENE 9

LUBIN, CHEVALIER

LUBIN: *(Calls from outside.)* Monsieur!… *(Then appears, looking very sad.)* What can I do for you, Monsieur?

CHEVALIER: What are you looking so sad about?

LUBIN: Alas! Monsieur, when I don't have anything to keep me busy, I grow sad thinking about your mistress, and a little thinking of mine: I'm upset that we're going away; but if we stayed, I'd be just as upset.

CHEVALIER: Well, we're not going, so forget the instructions I gave you.

LUBIN: We're not going!

CHEVALIER: No, I've changed my mind.

LUBIN: But, Monsieur, I've packed.

CHEVALIER: Well, then! Unpack.

LUBIN: But I've said goodbye to everyone for ever, how can I say hello to them again?

CHEVALIER: Eh! shut up; give me back my letters.

LUBIN: They're no bother, I'll deliver them presently.

CHEVALIER: You don't need to, now we're staying.

LUBIN: I don't understand anything; why waste good letters? But, Monsieur, who has stopped you from going, is it Madame the Marquise?

CHEVALIER: Yes.

LUBIN: And we're not moving house?

CHEVALIER: Why move?

LUBIN: Ah! That's me done for.

CHEVALIER: How so?

LUBIN: Your houses are neighbours; you can go from one straight into the other; I don't have my mistress any more; Madame the Marquise has a very agreeable chamber maid; from your house, I'll take two steps into hers and boom! That's me unfaithful, and it makes me feel bad. Poor Marton! Will I have to forget you?

CHEVALIER: You'd be displaying a very poor character.

LUBIN: Ah! that's true, yes, it would be very shameful of me, but that won't stop it happening: I'm already getting pleasant feelings, and they're throwing me into despair. Still, if you'd have the goodness to set me an example... Look out, it's her, Lisette!

SCENE 10

LISETTE, COUNT, CHEVALIER, LUBIN

COUNT: I was on my way to your place, Chevalier, but Lisette said you were here; she's told me of your misfortune, I hope you know how much I share your sorrows; we must do what we can to dispel them.

CHEVALIER: Not easy, Monsieur the Count.

LUBIN: *(Giving a sob.)* Eh!

CHEVALIER: Keep quiet.

COUNT: What's happened to this poor fellow?

CHEVALIER: He says he's upset because we're now not going away as I'd been planning.

LUBIN: *(Laughing.)* However I'm happy to stay put, on account of Lisette.

LISETTE: Such gallantry! But, Monsieur the Chevalier, to explain what's brought us here, Monsieur the Count and myself: I happened to be in the arbour during your conversation with Madame the Marquise, and without intending to, I heard part of what you were saying; my mistress has advised you to stay here, you've abandoned your journey, you're both unhappy and the similarity of your feelings mean that you'll often be meeting. I feel very close to my mistress, more than I know how to say, and it makes me wretched having to watch her not even trying to find some consolation, but going on and on with her weeping and sighing; she'll be indulging her grief until her very last breath. Don't encourage her in this, try if you can to draw her out of her melancholy: Monsieur the

Count here is in love with her, you know him, he's a friend of yours; Madame the Marquise is not averse to him calling on her; this would be a suitable marriage; I'm doing all I can to make it succeed; support us from your side, Monsieur the Chevalier, do a good turn for your friend, a good turn for my mistress, too.

CHEVALIER: But, Lisette, haven't you just this moment said that Madame the Marquise is not averse to the Count's visits?

COUNT: 'Not averse' means she puts up with me; that's all.

LISETTE: And receives your visits.

CHEVALIER: Indeed; but is she aware that you love her?

COUNT: I believe she is.

LISETTE: From time to time, on my part, I slip in a few little words, to make her take notice.

CHEVALIER: But those few little words, I'm sure, must make a big impact; you're in good hands, Monsieur the Count. And what does the Marquise say to you? Does she respond in a promising manner?

COUNT: So far, she's treated me most graciously.

CHEVALIER: Most graciously! Seriously?

COUNT: That's how it appears to me.

CHEVALIER: *(Abruptly.)* In that case, you don't have any need of me?

COUNT: I'm astonished how you draw that conclusion.

CHEVALIER: Not at all, I'm saying clearly: your love is noticed, your presence is accepted, you are made welcome most graciously, it's apparent that she likes you, and I might ruin the whole affair if I started to interfere; it will succeed on its own.

LISETTE: I swear I don't understand this line of reasoning at all.

COUNT: I'm as surprised as you.

CHEVALIER: Believe me, Monsieur the Count, I was only considering what was for the best; but since you insist, I'll speak to her, and whatever happens, happens, since you insist; despite my reservations, I'm still your servant and your friend.

COUNT: No, Monsieur, I'm very grateful to you, but you'll have the goodness to say nothing; I'll travel my own road. Goodbye, Lisette, don't forget about me; as your mistress is busy, I'll call back another time.

SCENE 11

CHEVALIER, LISETTE, LUBIN

CHEVALIER: Try to make people see reason, that's what happens. What a peculiar man, he took leave of me as coldly as if we were rivals.

LUBIN: Well, every cloud has a silver lining; it reminds you that you can't rely on anyone for ever, and you should never swear undying vows: that's just living in fairy land; I say stock up on the goods to hand and long live what's available! isn't that right, Lisette?

LISETTE: Monsieur the Chevalier, dare I speak openly to you?

CHEVALIER: Go ahead.

LISETTE: Mad'moiselle Angélique is lost to you.

CHEVALIER: I think I know that – rather too well.

LISETTE: Madame the Marquise is rich, young, beautiful.

LUBIN: She's a delicacy.

CHEVALIER: And?

LISETTE: Well, Monsieur, you've just seen her sighing in grief, don't you think she sighs charmingly? I believe you take my meaning?

LUBIN: Be daring, Monsieur.

CHEVALIER: Make yourself clear; are you implying that I have feelings towards her?

LISETTE: Why not? I could wish for that with all my heart; the state I see my mistress in, what does it matter who leads her out of it, if he's a decent man she marries?

LUBIN: That's well put; it would have to be a decent man, there'd be no chance of her marrying an indecent one.

CHEVALIER: *(Coldly.)* If you have anything to add, Lisette.

LISETTE: Well, Monsieur, on the subject of grieving, weren't you about to entomb yourself in some solitude, never to be heard of again? If only you knew, at this moment, how perfectly your countenance belongs in a wilderness, you'd have the gratification of finding nothing there that looked half so miserable. Believe me, Monsieur, apathy, exhaustion, desolation, despair, all varnished with unsociability, that's the gloomy portrait currently representing your face; I'm convinced the sight of it might well cause people to fall sick; you should hesitate before you parade it in public. And that's not all: when you speak, you sound like someone about to gasp their dying sigh; you drag out your words, they're paralysing, like a poisonous chill that numbs the soul, I can feel mine beginning to congeal this minute, and I've had quite enough of it; do take some pity on us. Not that I'm blaming you; you've lost your mistress, you've dedicated yourself to grief, you've expressed the wish to die; well done, that will be an edification for the entire world; they will speak of you in history, you'll be an excellent example worth citing; but to have to look you in the face at the present moment, no thank you; have the goodness to edify us from further off.

CHEVALIER:	Lisette, I forgive your ardour on behalf of your mistress; but I don't care for your choice of words.
LUBIN:	They're uncouth.
CHEVALIER:	I've just cancelled my departure; I've no intention of changing my mind every five minutes, so I will not be going away. Concerning the Count, I shall speak to your mistress in his favour; and if it's true, as I predict, that she has a *penchant* for him, don't worry about a thing, my visits will be infrequent, and my unhappiness will spoil nothing.
LISETTE:	That's all you have to say to me, Monsieur?
CHEVALIER:	What else should I possibly say?
LISETTE:	Good morning, Monsieur; your servant.

SCENE 12

LUBIN, CHEVALIER

CHEVALIER:	*(In thought for a while.)* Everything I've heard here makes the loss of Angélique even more painful.
LUBIN:	Believe me, Angélique's a pain in the neck.
CHEVALIER:	*(Pacing to and fro.)* I was expecting to find some consolation from the Marquise, her brave resolve never to love again made her worthy of respect; and here she is about to remarry; and soon: I thought her different, she's just like any other woman.
LUBIN:	Put yourself in the place of a widow who feels totally at a loss.
CHEVALIER:	Ah! My dearest Angélique, if there were one thing in the world that could bring me consolation, it's to see how far you are above your sex, how much more than deserving of my devotion.

25

LUBIN: Ah! Marton! Marton! I was cheerfully on my way to forgetting you; but my master doesn't want me to complete that journey; so I'm on my way back to missing you as I did before, heaven have pity on me!…

CHEVALIER: *(Still pacing.)* I feel more worn down than ever by my unhappiness.

LUBIN: Lisette did cheer me up a little.

CHEVALIER: I shall shut myself in the house; I'll just see the Marquise on occasion, I have no purpose here if she marries: I'll be too upset to witness the festivities! Really, the Marquise, what is she thinking of? What's become of her husband's memory?

LUBIN: Ah! Monsieur, what d'you expect her to do with a memory?

CHEVALIER: As it stands, I promised to have my books sent over, so I'll do what I said if only out of decency. Go and look for the man who's taking care of them: wouldn't this be him coming?

SCENE 13

HORTENSIUS, LUBIN, CHEVALIER

HORTENSIUS: I have the honour of making myself known to you, Monsieur, my name is Hortensius. Madame the Marquise whose reading I have the pleasure of directing, and whom I am also teaching, in turn, literature, morality and philosophy, without disregard for all the other disciplines I could teach her, gives me to understand, Monsieur, that you wish to show me your library, which will no doubt bear witness to the excellence of your taste; in which case, Monsieur, when would you like this to happen?

CHEVALIER:	Lubin will take you to my library, Monsieur, and can bring the books back here for you.
HORTENSIUS:	It will be taken care of as you request.

SCENE 14

HORTENSIUS, LUBIN

HORTENSIUS:	Well, my lad, I wait on you.
LUBIN:	A brief moment's word, Monsieur Dr Hortus.
HORTENSIUS:	Hortensius, Hortensius; don't disfigure my name.
LUBIN:	No, no, keep it as it is, I didn't mean to spoil its shape.
HORTENSIUS:	*(Aside.)* He seems sincere; but what's to be done, one must gain the goodwill of everyone.
LUBIN:	You teach morality and philosophy to the Marquise.
HORTENSIUS:	Yes.
LUBIN:	What use do they serve, these things?…
HORTENSIUS:	To purge the soul of its passions.
LUBIN:	All the better, doctor; show me how to take a draught of this medicine against melancholy.
HORTENSIUS:	Are you unhappy then?
LUBIN:	Unhappy! I'd probably be dead, if it wasn't for my big appetite.
HORTENSIUS:	You have a powerful antidote there: however, I will say this to you, that unhappiness is always useless because it cures nothing, reason must be the rule in every situation.
LUBIN:	Don't talk to me about reason, I know all there is to know on that subject; what about some of your morality to purge me.
HORTENSIUS:	By all means, that's the best.
LUBIN:	But maybe it won't suit my temperament; serve me up some philosophy.
HORTENSIUS:	They are more or less the same thing.

LUBIN:	What about literature then?
HORTENSIUS:	That certainly won't suit your temperament: but what is the nature of your unhappiness?
LUBIN:	It's love.
HORTENSIUS:	Oh! philosophy is against falling in love.
LUBIN:	Yes; but if you've already fallen, then what?
HORTENSIUS:	You must renounce it, give it up.
LUBIN:	Give it up? But what if it won't let go? Because it can run after you.
HORTENSIUS:	You must fly from it with all your strength.
LUBIN:	Fine! But when you're in love, do you have legs to run away on? Does philosophy provide them?
HORTENSIUS:	Philosophy provides us with excellent advice.
LUBIN:	Advice? Ah! not the best vehicle for a getaway!
HORTENSIUS:	Listen, do you want an infallible method? While you're weeping over one mistress, get yourself another.
LUBIN:	Eh, good heavens, you don't say so? That's good advice, that is. I'll bet that's the morality you've been serving up to the Marquise, seeing she's about to marry Monsieur the Count?
HORTENSIUS:	*(Stunned.)* Did you say she's getting married?
LUBIN:	Definitely; and if we'd wanted her, we could have had first choice, Lisette offered her to us.
HORTENSIUS:	Are you absolutely certain of what you're saying?
LUBIN:	On the grounds that Lisette then suggested that we withdraw, because we were so miserable, and you were a bit on the pedantic side, that's what she said, and that the Marquise had to be made happy.
HORTENSIUS:	*(Aside.) Bene, bene, O, Fortuna,* I give you thanks for this discovery! I've found a comfortable nest here, and this marriage

	would toss me out of it, but I shall stir up so much turbulence, there'll be no one able to withstand the storm.
LUBIN:	What are you mumbling behind your teeth, Doctor?
HORTENSIUS:	Nothing; let's get on with collecting those books, *tempus fugit.*

End of Act One.

ACT 2

SCENE 1

LUBIN, HORTENSIUS

LUBIN: *(Laden with a hamper of books on which he sits.)* Talk about the weight of knowledge!

HORTENSIUS: A soufflé. I carry far more books in my head than those under your backside.

LUBIN: You do?

HORTENSIUS: I do indeed.

LUBIN: Then you're bookshop and bookseller all in one. And what d'you do with all those books in your head?

HORTENSIUS: I nourish my intellect.

LUBIN: They don't seem to do much for it; a bit on the thin side, if you ask me.

HORTENSIUS: You're no judge of such matters. But now you've got yourself seated, take a moment's rest, then look for me in the library, I'll be making space for these.

LUBIN: Go ahead, always ahead.

SCENE 2

LISETTE, LUBIN

LUBIN: *(Alone for a moment.)* Ah! Poor Lubin! Your heart's really rent in twain; I now just don't know if it's Marton I love any more, or Lisette; I think it might be Lisette, at least if it's not Marton.

LISETTE: *(Entering with LA BRIE carrying chairs.)* Bring them in, one or two more and put them over there.

LUBIN: Hello, my love.

LISETTE:	What on earth are you doing here?
LUBIN:	Resting on a pile of books I've just carried over to nourish your mistress's intellect, or so the learnèd Doctor makes out.
LISETTE:	They nourish her stupidity, if you ask me! When are we going to see the end of this lunacy? Take that pile of pretentious paperwork with you and be off.
LUBIN:	Excuse me, it's full of morality and philosophy; they're supposed to purge the soul of its passions. I tried a small dose, but it only made me sneeze.
LISETTE:	I don't know what you're babbling about, leave me in peace, just go.
LUBIN:	Eh! so you didn't have the chairs brought here for me?
LISETTE:	You numbskull! They're for Madame, and she'll soon be here.
LUBIN:	While you're waiting, can I trouble you to sit down, Mad'moiselle, just for a moment? I'm asking nicely, I've got something to communicate to you.
LISETTE:	Well, what d'you want with me, Monsieur ?
LUBIN:	In confidence, Lisette, I've been taking a good look at what's going on in my heart, and I see Marton's face moving out, and yours trying to move in: I've told it I'd discuss it with you, it's waiting: d'you think I should let it in?
LISETTE:	No, Lubin, I advise you to send it away; what would you do with it? What could it lead to? What use would it serve us to love one another.
LUBIN:	Ah! Lovers can always make love work to their advantage.
LISETTE:	I'm telling you no; your master isn't interested in linking himself to my mistress

	and my place in life's totally dependent on hers, just as yours is on his.
LUBIN:	That's true; I'd forgotten – my fate's weighted against me looking in your direction. Even so, if you did find me to your liking, it'd be a shame for you not to be free to enjoy your liking; opportunities like this don't happen every day: would you be agreeable to me dropping a hint to the Marquise? She's great friends with the Chevalier, so's he with her; it wouldn't be that hard for them to shift from friendship to marriage, that would sort us out in a flash.
LISETTE:	Shush. Here is Madame.
LUBIN:	Leave it to me.

SCENE 3

MARQUISE, HORTENSIUS, LUBIN, LISETTE

MARQUISE:	Lisette, go and tell them I'm not in to anyone, I think this is the hour for our reading, we ought to let the Chevalier know. Ah! you're there, Lubin, where's your master?
LUBIN:	I think he went home, Madame, to do some sighing.
MARQUISE:	Go and tell him we're waiting for him.
LUBIN:	Yes, Madame: and I'll also have a small trifle to propose to you, which I'll take the liberty to discuss with you in all humility, as is right and proper.
MARQUISE:	Eh! What is it about?
LUBIN:	Oh! almost nothing; we'll talk about it after I've delivered your message.
MARQUISE:	I'm at your service, if I can be.

SCENE 4

HORTENSIUS, MARQUISE

MARQUISE: *(Casually.)* Well, Monsieur, so you don't much care for the Chevalier's choice of books?

HORTENSIUS: No, Madame, the selection appears to lack erudition; in six volumes not the least reference to our classic authors, who should provide the entire essence of a writer's work; in short, these are merely modern books filled with witticisms; always wit, nothing but wit, triviality that offends against reason.

MARQUISE: *(Still casual.)* But wit! Didn't the Greeks and Romans have any?

HORTENSIUS: Ah! Madame, *distinguo* – I make the distinction, they had wit but in a manner… oh! In a manner that I find admirable.

MARQUISE: Explain this manner to me.

HORTENSIUS: I find it difficult to decide which image to choose as an example, for it is indeed by images that the Ancients painted their thoughts. Here's how a modern author describes their wit; I've retained his words: Imagine for yourself, he says, a woman of fashion: *primo*, her dress is à la mode, all slashes, frills and furbelows; instead of beauty, she has beauty-spots, instead of smiles, we get pouts; she doesn't gesture, she gesticulates; she doesn't look, she leers; she doesn't observe, she ogles, she doesn't walk, she waddles; she doesn't charm, she coquettes; she doesn't occupy her time, she passes it. She is considered elegant, but I find her ridiculous: and it is this presumptuous woman whom the wits of today resemble, so says our author.

MARQUISE: I take the point completely.

HORTENSIUS: By contrast, he goes on to say, the wit of the ancient writers, ah! it is of such a male beauty, that in order to discern it, you have to question whether it actually exists; modest in its manner, you could not say it thrusts itself at the world; but only make the effort in all goodwill to warm to it, and you will discover its charm.

MARQUISE: That's more than enough. I understand you; we moderns are overrefined, those ancients were underdeveloped.

HORTENSIUS: Heaven forfend! Madame, Hortensius had no intention…

MARQUISE: Why don't we change the subject; what are you reading for us today?

HORTENSIUS: I'd decided on something from *The Treatise on Patience*, the opening chapter on Widowhood.

MARQUISE: Oh! choose something else; nothing makes me more impatient than pieces on patience.

HORTENSIUS: Your statement doesn't entirely surprise me.

MARQUISE: I'd prefer *In Praise of Friendship*, we could read something from that.

HORTENSIUS: I'll entreat you to disburden me of that, Madame, it's hardly worth the effort in the short time that remains available for us, now that you're marrying Monsieur the Count.

MARQUISE: Me!

HORTENSIUS: Yes, Madame, as a consequence of which, I have now become an unnecessary employee, somewhat similar to troops that you provide for in wartime and disband in peace. I have been battling with your passions, but now you've made a truce with them, I withdraw my service before I'm discharged.

MARQUISE: You make pretty speeches with your passions, and you're right to make us wary of them, but I don't need you to battle with mine; passions

I've made a truce with! Really, you're ludicrous. And this marriage, where did you get that from?

HORTENSIUS: From Mademoiselle Lisette who told Lubin, who reported it to me, with this unfavourable footnote that this marriage would drive me onto the streets.

MARQUISE: *(Astonished.)* What is this all about? The Chevalier will think I've gone mad. I want to know how he reacted, don't hold anything back, speak.

HORTENSIUS: Madame, I know nothing about that, it's all somewhat vague.

MARQUISE: Vague, that's highly informative; let's hear this vagueness.

HORTENSIUS: I believe that Lisette only told the Chevalier you were planning to marry the Count in order to…

MARQUISE: Spare me the details.

HORTENSIUS: …in order to discover if the said Chevalier would try to seek you out himself and substitute himself for the said Count; and it further appears in the account of the said Lubin, that the said Lisette offered your hand to the aforesaid Chevalier.

MARQUISE: Dear God, what you're telling me is inconceivable, to offer a woman's hand here, there and everywhere, and to say to all and sundry: Do you want it? Ah! ah! I can see the Chevalier retreating ten paces at the proposition, can't you?

HORTENSIUS: I'm searching for his exact response.

MARQUISE: No plunging into confusion, Monsieur, you usually have an extremely precise memory.

HORTENSIUS: The account goes that he first cried out in amazement, and then he declined the offer.

MARQUISE:	Oh! cried out, you say! He might have had a little self-control, I find that utterly discourteous and, worse, indiscreet; however, I do approve the spirit of it, if he'd responded affirmatively, I'd never again have tolerated him in my life. But to decline my hand in front of the servants, to expose me to their mockery – ah! that's a little *de trop*, there is no situation that exempts a man from conducting himself decently.
HORTENSIUS:	Your critical assessment is judicious, Madame.
MARQUISE:	Oh! I assure you I will sort this out; how can this be? it's a direct attack on me, it's virtually contempt. Oh, Chevalier, love your Angélique as much as you wish, but don't make me suffer for it, if you don't mind! I may not want to marry, but that doesn't mean I want to be refused.
HORTENSIUS:	What you say is beyond argument. *(Aside.)* This is going well. *(To the MARQUISE.)* But, Madame, what will become of me? May I remain here? Have I nothing to fear?
MARQUISE:	Come, Monsieur, I shall retain you for the next hundred years, you have neither the Count nor the Chevalier to fear, I'm assuring you of that myself, you're under my protection. Take up your book, let's read, I'm not expecting anyone. *(HORTENSIUS takes up a book.)*

SCENE 5

LUBIN, HORTENSIUS, MARQUISE

LUBIN:	Madame, Monsieur the Chevalier's been unexpectedly delayed, he's on his way and says to expect him.
MARQUISE:	Yes, yes, we'll expect him when he gets here.

LUBIN: If you would permit me a moment now, Madame, I'd request the honour of that brief word with you.

MARQUISE: Well, what is it? Go on.

LUBIN: Oh! I don't think I dare, you look angry.

MARQUISE: *(To HORTENSIUS.)* I, angry? Do I look angry, Monsieur?

HORTENSIUS: Peace rules your demeanour.

LUBIN: But war might break out.

MARQUISE: Say what you have to say.

LUBIN: You're possibly aware that Lisette finds my person quite to her liking, as mine finds hers, and it would be a foregone conclusion if, by a generosity of heart that would complete our happiness, Madame, who is herself thinking of marrying, would try to feel a little love for my master; he is at all times worthy of esteem, but in this circumstance he would conduct himself with utterly appropriate seemliness.

MARQUISE: *(To HORTENSIUS.)* Aha! Did you hear that, this confirms a lot of what you've been telling me.

LUBIN: There's also talk of Monsieur the Count; now counts are very decent men, I respect them a lot, but, if I were a woman, I'd rather have chevaliers for a husband: long live a junior officer in the household!

MARQUISE: His enthusiasm's appealing. I agree with you, Lubin, but sadly, as I'm given to understand, your master doesn't much care for me.

LUBIN: It's true, he doesn't love you, and we've been telling him off about it, me and Lisette, but if you gave him a bit of encouragement, that might set things rolling.

MARQUISE: *(To HORTENSIUS.)* Well, Monsieur, what have you to say? Do you see what sort of role I'm forced to play in all this? The Chevalier's stupidity – it's making me look utterly ridiculous.

HORTENSIUS: With your great sagacity, you saw this coming.

LUBIN: Oh! I don't dispute he's made a stupid mistake, but when that happens, a decent man puts things right.

MARQUISE: Hold your tongue, that's quite enough from you.

LUBIN: Alas! Madame, I'd be very upset if I upset you, all I beg of you is to give it some thought.

SCENE 6

LISETTE, LUBIN, MARQUISE, HORTENSIUS

LISETTE: I've just passed on your orders, Madame, they'll say you're not at home, but a moment after…

MARQUISE: Enough about that, other matters concern me at the moment; come here, now; *(To LUBIN.)* and you, stay there, if you please.

LISETTE: What's this about then? All this formality?

LUBIN: *(Quietly to LISETTE.)* You're about to hear of my endeavours.

MARQUISE: My marriage to the Count, Lisette, when do you plan to finalise it?

LISETTE: *(Looking towards LUBIN.)* You blunderer.

LUBIN: Listen, listen.

MARQUISE: Answer me then, when do you plan to finalise it? *(HORTENSIUS laughs.)*

LISETTE: *(Bluffing.)* Eh, eh, eh. Why are you asking me that?

MARQUISE: Because it's just come to my ears that you're marrying me off to the Count, on the defection of the Chevalier, to whom you offered me in the first place, but who is not in the least interested in me, in spite of all you put to him, you and his valet, who himself has been exhorting me to demonstrate some attraction for his master in the hope that this will change his mind.

LISETTE: I'm amazed by the turn things take, even the best-intentioned, when reported by an idiot.

LUBIN: I'm the one referred to, I think?

MARQUISE: You're amazed by the turn things take?

LISETTE: Ah now, Madame, you're not about to get worked up, are you? You surely don't think I did anything wrong?

MARQUISE: What, you'd carry your effrontery that far, Lisette! What, begging the Chevalier to do me the favour of loving me, so you can marry that imbecile over there!

LUBIN: Always me, always me.

MARQUISE: And what's all this about the Count being in love with me? You appear to have the ear of any man whose heart's inclined towards me, about which I know absolutely nothing, correct? Unimaginable! Here I am still prone to tears, and my hand and heart are being proffered around to any man who's available, even those who don't want them; I suffer rejections, I endure affronts, I have lovers, of whom I'm totally ignorant, confident of success? A woman in a situation like mine deserves the greatest commiseration! How demeaned I am, how far I've fallen!

LUBIN: *(Aside.)* And that's our future taking a tumble.

MARQUISE: Really, I thought you had more devotion and more respect for your mistress.

LISETTE: Indeed, Madame, you may well speak of devotion, I've paid for mine: this is how it is when you devote yourself to a mistress, no gratitude, no recognition; succeed in serving them well and all the advantage is theirs; not so successful, and they treat you like rubbish.

LUBIN: Like imbeciles.

HORTENSIUS: *(To LISETTE.)* It must be said it would have been better had none of this occurred.

MARQUISE: Eh! Monsieur, my widowhood is for life; in fact, there's no woman alive further from marriage than I; I've lost the only man who could ever please me; but despite that, a woman still finds herself open to disagreeable advances. Well, really, the Chevalier has refused my hand: my self-esteem doesn't think ill of him for that; but, as I've already told you, the tone, the manner in which he did so is what I condemn. If he had actually loved me, it would of course have been futile for him. But he did indeed refuse me, that's an established fact, and he could boast about it, he may well do so, and what would come of that? It casts a woman in the rags of an outcast, the regard and interest to which she's accustomed begin to fade, people's minds are cooled towards her, I don't even talk of their hearts! Little of that, however, concerns me: nevertheless a woman needs some consideration in life, we depend on the opinion of others, reputation endows us with everything, and reputation deprives us of everything, so much so that if, after all that's happened to me, I should ever wish to remarry – I'm merely supposing of course – I will have sunk so low in people's estimation that it would hardly enhance the standing of any suitor to woo me; the Count – I'm sure of it – he'd want nothing to do with me.

LUBIN: *(From the back.)* It wouldn't put me off.

LISETTE:	And I, Madame, I say the Chevalier's a hypocrite, for if his refusal was so definite, why didn't he want to help Monsieur the Count, when I asked him? Why did he refuse so firmly and in such an agitated manner, he looked distinctly nettled.
MARQUISE:	What do you mean, agitated? What? What are you trying to say? That he was jealous? This is quite a different story.
LISETTE:	Yes, Madame, he looked jealous to me: that's how it was; his whole demeanour showed it. Monsieur knows how the Count feels about you, how you receive him; he was told you accept his visits, that you treat him most graciously: 'Most graciously', he says, full of resentment, 'then it's hardly worth my getting involved?' Who wouldn't have thought he was thinking of you for himself? That's why I said what I said: eh! who knows what goes in anyone's head? That he does love you, perhaps!
LUBIN:	*(Behind.)* He's more than capable of it.
MARQUISE:	Look at me, I've lost my bearings, I know no longer how to comport myself; there must be a way, but I've no idea what it is, I'm utterly disorientated.
HORTENSIUS:	If you would permit me, Madame, I shall teach you a little axiom, which will be splendidly instructive for you, it is that the jealous person always pursues what he desires: now, it being manifestly clear that the Chevalier rejects you…
MARQUISE:	Rejects me! You express yourself crudely, your axiom doesn't know what it's talking about, and it's not at all certain that he has rejected me.
LISETTE:	Far from it; ask the Count what he thinks.
MARQUISE:	What, don't tell me the Count was present?

LISETTE: Not for long; he simply thought the Chevalier was behaving like a rival.

MARQUISE: That's not enough, that he thought it so, it's not enough, it has to be so; nothing but that can avenge – repair – the insult of what's virtually a public rejection, nothing but that. For me to get reparation, his outburst has to have been from lover's pique. To need a lover's spite to right a wrong! That must make you laugh? Surely. It isn't that I'm in any way concerned with what's commonly called a woman's honour, stupid, ridiculous honour, but it's established, accepted, as something we have to maintain, to be our protection, our adornment. That's how men think, so we have to think like men in order to live amongst them. What becomes of my honour if the Chevalier isn't jealous? Well, is he? Isn't he? I have no idea, maybe it's maybe: but my honour is harmed by it, stupid, ridiculous as it is, so here I am, in the pathetic necessity of being loved by a man I don't care for; but how to deal with it? Oh! I will not put up with it, I will not. I will not tolerate it. What do you say, sir? I absolutely have to clarify this matter.

HORTENSIUS: The complete solution, Madame, is contempt.

MARQUISE: Eh, no, Monsieur, your advice is futile; you only know how to read books.

LUBIN: I see a beating for me in all this.

LISETTE: *(Weeping.)* As for me, Madame, I don't know what's getting you in such a state; anyone would think I'd turned the whole world upside down. No maid has ever loved her mistress the way I love you: I look for ways to help you, and then I discover that I've committed every wrong imaginable. I can't carry on like this; I'd rather withdraw from

your service, that way I won't see your
unhappiness anymore, and the desire to
help you won't make me commit any more
effronteries.

MARQUISE: It's not about your tears; I am compromised
and I can see no end to it. Aha, here's the
Chevalier, don't go, I need witnesses.

SCENE 7

CHEVALIER, MARQUISE, LISETTE, LUBIN, HORTENSIUS

CHEVALIER: You may have been expecting me, Madame,
my apologies, business…

MARQUISE: No harm done, Monsieur the Chevalier, a
reading delayed, nothing more.

CHEVALIER: Besides, I thought Monsieur the Count was
keeping you company and that made me feel
easier.

LUBIN: *(Aside.)* Ugh-ugh! I'm off.

MARQUISE: *(Scrutinising the CHEVALIER closely.)* I was told
you'd seen him yourself, the Count.

CHEVALIER: Yes, Madame.

MARQUISE: *(Always watching him.)* He's a very decent
man.

CHEVALIER: Without a doubt, and has, so I believe, the
perfect temperament for consoling those in
need of consolation.

MARQUISE: He's a firm friend of mine.

CHEVALIER: Mine, also.

MARQUISE: I didn't know you were so well acquainted;
he calls here from time to time, he's almost
the only one of my late husband's friends
I still see; to me, he seems worthy of that
distinction, don't you agree?

CHEVALIER: Yes, Madame, you're correct, I think like you;
he deserves to be singled out.

MARQUISE: *(Quietly to LISETTE.)* You find this man jealous, Lisette?

CHEVALIER: *(Aside.)* Monsieur and his merits are beginning to try my patience. *(To the MARQUISE.)* Madame, you mentioned a reading, if, as it seems, I'm disturbing your arrangements, I really ought to withdraw.

MARQUISE: Since this conversation appears to be trying your patience, why don't we start the reading.

CHEVALIER: You express your concern for my patience very strangely.

MARQUISE: Not at all, and you'll enjoy it. *(To LISETTE.)* Take yourself away, Lisette, you're getting on my nerves standing there. *(To HORTENSIUS.)* And you, Monsieur, I'll call you back, don't wander off too far. *(To the CHEVALIER.)* As for you, Chevalier, I still need a word with you before we read; it's a little matter of clarification that doesn't concern you, it only affects me, and I ask the favour of your answering the question I'm about to put to you with the utmost straightforwardness.

CHEVALIER: Here I am, Madame, listening to you.

MARQUISE: I've just found out that the Count loves me, I had no idea.

CHEVALIER: *(Ironically.)* You had no idea!

MARQUISE: Don't imply I'm not speaking the truth, and don't interrupt me.

CHEVALIER: Then it's a very peculiar truth.

MARQUISE: There's nothing I can do about that, it is what it is; of course bad-humoured persons may take it as they wish.

CHEVALIER: I do apologise for speaking my mind, do go on.

MARQUISE: *(Impatiently.)* You're making me lose patience! Did you exhibit this disposition to Angélique? She can hardly have found it pleasing.

CHEVALIER:	It's the only one I have, but it was to her liking, unluckily not to yours; that's the big difference.
MARQUISE:	You did at least listen to her when she spoke to you; so now you can listen to me. Lisette asked you to speak to me on behalf of the Count, but you refused.
CHEVALIER:	Why would I do something so pointless: the Count is a suitor, you made it clear to me you were no longer interested in suitors; but of course you are your own mistress.
MARQUISE:	True, I am no longer interested; now, tell me, in your opinion, can one respond to the love of a man one doesn't care for? You're very peculiar.
CHEVALIER:	Ha, ha, ha, I admire the effort you're making to hide your feelings: you're afraid I'll criticise them after everything you've said to me; but no, Madame, you mustn't feel embarrassed; I know how much it costs to reckon with the human heart, I see nothing peculiar in that, nothing out of the ordinary.
MARQUISE:	*(Angrily.)* No, I've never in my life had such a desire to quarrel with someone. Good day.
CHEVALIER:	*(Stopping her.)* Ah! Marquise, this is only a conversation, I'd be wretched if I upset you; please do finish what you wish to ask me.
MARQUISE:	As I was saying. You're the most estimable man in the world, when it suits you; and I have no idea what chance occurrence today has put you so out of character, you're naturally civil and reasonable; allow me to finish… I don't know where I got to.
CHEVALIER:	To the Count, whom you don't care for.
MARQUISE:	Oh, yes, the Count I don't care for, on whose behalf you didn't wish to intervene with me;

	Lisette even thought you looked somewhat nettled.
CHEVALIER:	There could be something in that.
MARQUISE:	I'll take that for a reply, and I'm grateful; from your discomposure, she got the impression that you might not find me totally to your disliking.
CHEVALIER:	*(Bows laughing.)* That's hardly a difficult impression to get.
MARQUISE:	Why? One woman can't be to the liking of everyone, but because she felt you were in harmony with me, she offered you my hand – as if the offer were hers to make! It's true, I've often allowed her far too much freedom in my affairs; she told me that you recoiled in disdain at the proposition.
CHEVALIER:	Recoiled in disdain? I call that sheer fantasy, beyond imagination.
MARQUISE:	Stay calm, here is my question: did you reject Lisette's offer out of resentment at the Count's interest in me; or out of pure disgust at the offer itself? Was it jealous pique? – After all, despite our pact, your heart could have been tempted by mine – or was it indeed true disdain?
CHEVALIER:	Let's start by eliminating the latter, it's inconceivable; as for jealousy…
MARQUISE:	Speak bluntly.
CHEVALIER:	*(At a loss.)* What would you say if I found that to be the case?
MARQUISE:	I would say… You were jealous.
CHEVALIER:	Yes, but, Madame, would you forgive me for what you so hate?
MARQUISE:	Then you weren't so at all? *(She looks at him.)* I understand you, I predicted as much, and my injury is confirmed.

CHEVALIER:	Why do you speak of injury? Where is it? Have I offended you?
MARQUISE:	Offended, Chevalier? no, certainly not, why should you offend me? You don't understand me at all, it's Lisette's impertinence that angers me: I had no part in the offer she made you, you have to know that, that is all; however by all means feel indifference to me, or aversion, what does it matter to me, I prefer those to love, and at least, you wouldn't be making a mistake.
CHEVALIER:	Who me, Madame, make a mistake! Come! It was your frame of mind when we met that drew me to you: you know that perfectly well, and since the loss of Angélique, I'd almost forgotten the possibility of love – if you hadn't just spoken of it.
MARQUISE:	Oh! in my case, I can speak of it without reminding myself of it. *(Calling.)* Come, Monsieur Hortensius, come and take your place, read me something cheerful, something diverting.

SCENE 8

HORTENSIUS, MARQUISE, CHEVALIER

MARQUISE:	Chevalier, it's entirely your decision, stay if our reading appeals to you, but you look filled with gloom and I'm attempting to dispel mine.
CHEVALIER:	*(Gravely.)* I, myself, Madame, I'm not yet ready for light-hearted readings. *(He goes.)*
MARQUISE:	What is the book?
HORTENSIUS:	These are extremely serious reflections.
MARQUISE:	Well, why didn't you speak up, you're very taciturn, letting the Chevalier leave, when what you're going to read would suit his mood?

HORTENSIUS:	Monsieur the Chevalier! Monsieur the Chevalier!
CHEVALIER:	*(Returning.)* What is it?
HORTENSIUS:	Madame begs you to come back, I shan't be reading anything too recreational.
MARQUISE:	What do you mean: Madame begs you? I'm not in the least begging; you have this book of reflections...and you called Monsieur back, that's all.
CHEVALIER:	I'm aware of acting improperly, Madame, by withdrawing, I'll stay if you'd like me to?
MARQUISE:	Whatever you please; shall we sit down then. *(They take their seats.)*
HORTENSIUS:	*(Clears his throat, then begins to read.)* 'Reason has a value before which all else surrenders; it is reason that provides our true greatness; with reason one is naturally endowed with all the virtues, so that, finally, the worthiest man is not the most powerful, but the most rational.'
CHEVALIER:	*(Shifting in his seat.)* Well, on that footing, the worthiest man can be nothing but an illusion; when I say man, I mean mankind, of course.
MARQUISE:	But some people at least are more rational than others.
CHEVALIER:	Hum! Let's say less stupid, that's safer.
MARQUISE:	Eh! please allow me a little reason, Chevalier, I wouldn't want to admit to stupidity.
CHEVALIER:	You, Madame, eh! surely you're the exception? that goes without saying, but this is the general rule.
MARQUISE:	I'll resist the temptation to thank you; let's go on.
HORTENSIUS:	'Since reason exerts so great a good, we must neglect nothing to preserve it, therefore let us take flight from the passions which rob us of reason; love is one of these...'

CHEVALIER: Love, love strips us of reason? that's not true; I was never more rational than when I loved Angélique, excessively so.

MARQUISE: You may be as rational as you please, that's your business, and no one's going to ask you to quantify it; but the author isn't entirely wrong, I myself know people made surly and uncivilised by love, and I don't think these defects embellish anyone.

HORTENSIUS: If Monsieur would give me permission to complete...

CHEVALIER: Trivial author, shallow intellect...

HORTENSIUS: *(Rising.)* Trivial author, shallow intellect! A man who cites Seneca to vouch for what he says, as you'll see further in folio twenty-four, chapter five.

CHEVALIER: Chapter one thousand, for all I care. Seneca doesn't know what he's talking about.

HORTENSIUS: This is untenable.

MARQUISE: *(Laughing.)* This is really more entertaining than my reading: but, Monsieur Hortensius, enough for now, the Chevalier doesn't care for your book at all. Let's not read any further, another time we'll be more in the mood.

CHEVALIER: Your taste, Madame, has to decide.

MARQUISE: My taste wants very much to be in harmony with yours.

HORTENSIUS: *(Leaving.)* Seneca, a trivial author! By Jupiter! if I were to say such a thing, I believe I'd be committing a literary blasphemy.

CHEVALIER: Servant, servant.

SCENE 9

MARQUISE, CHEVALIER

MARQUISE: There now, you've fallen out with Hortensius, Chevalier, what on earth made you slander Seneca?

CHEVALIER: I couldn't care less about Seneca and his advocates, just so long as you don't take their part, Madame.

MARQUISE: Ah! I'll remain neutral, in case the quarrel goes on, but I don't imagine you'll want to restart it; our pastimes bore you, don't they?

CHEVALIER: You'd need to be in a much calmer state than I am before you managed to find anything entertaining.

MARQUISE: Don't be concerned, Chevalier, we don't stand on ceremony here; you'd probably prefer to be on your own, I'll say adieu and leave you in peace.

CHEVALIER: There isn't a single circumstance that doesn't weigh on me.

MARQUISE: I wish with all my heart I could calm your spirits. *(She starts to leave.)*

CHEVALIER: Ah! I was expecting more peace of mind when I changed my plans; I shan't be making any more, I can see I just offend everyone.

MARQUISE: *(Stopping.)* I'm touched by what he's saying, it would be ungracious to leave him in this mood. *(She returns.)* No, Chevalier, you don't offend me; don't give in to your unhappiness: from the moment you responded to my sorrow, you were sensitive to the concern I took in yours, why isn't it the same for you now? That's what actually offends me, true friendship wants only to comfort and console.

CHEVALIER: It could also have had such an influence over me: if I had found friendship, no one in the world would have been more responsive to it;

my heart was primed for it, but what became of it? I believed I'd found it, how mistaken I was, and not without some cost to my heart!

MARQUISE: Could there be any reproach more unjust than the one that you've just made to me? What are you complaining about? Come now; about something of which you yourself were the cause: a maladroit servant offers you my hand, you find it repugnant, very well, that's not what shocks me; a man who has loved Angélique could well find all other women inferior, she may have affected his vision; besides, what's called vanity, I'm no longer prey to that.

CHEVALIER: Ah! Madame, I do mourn the loss of Angélique, but you might have consoled me, had you wished.

MARQUISE: I don't have much evidence of that: your repugnance, which of itself I don't complain, was it necessary to display it quite so openly? Look at this behaviour of yours with a cool head; you're an honourable man, but judge for yourself, where was the friendship you speak of then? For I say once again, I am not seeking love and you know that perfectly well, but doesn't friendship have its own sentiments, its own delicacies of feeling? Love has great tenderness, Chevalier, well, friendship is even more scrupulous than love in the way it cares for those it brings together; that's the portrait of it I've always painted in my mind, that's how I feel it to be, and how you should feel it: in my opinion, one cannot diminish its virtues and you seem to have no understanding of its obligations in the way I do: if someone were to offer your hand to me, for example, I would teach you the right way to respond.

CHEVALIER: Oh! I'm sure you'd have been even more
embarrassed than I was; after all, you were
never going to accept such an offer.

MARQUISE: Well, it never happened, that someone didn't
appear, and it isn't for you to tell me how I'd
have dealt with you: meanwhile, you're still
complaining.

CHEVALIER: Dear Heaven, Madame, you used the word
repugnance, and I wouldn't want you to suffer
from that misconception, so let me resolve it
once and for all; if I hadn't loved Angélique,
whom somehow I really must forget, you'd
have had only one thing to fear from me:
that my friendship might turn to love, and
rationally, as things stand, there isn't even
that to fear; that's all the repugnance I'm
aware of.

MARQUISE: Ah!, that, that could never have happened,
Chevalier, absolutely not, absolutely not.

CHEVALIER: But it would have paid you a just compliment.
Anyway, what was the cause of this rejection
you accuse me of? After all, wasn't it only
natural? The Count was in love with you,
you more than tolerated his presence; I was
beside myself to see his love trample across
a relationship that was meant to bring me
some consolation; my friendship wasn't
compatible with that, ours was supposed to be
a friendship unlike any other.

MARQUISE: Ah! that puts everything in a new light, I
retract my accusations, I'm satisfied; what
you say to me, I feel it, I sense it, it's precisely
the friendship I ask for, there it is, genuine,
delicate, jealous, and with every right to be
so; but why didn't you say anything to me?
Why didn't you come to me and say: What
is this Count to you? What is he doing in
your house? I would have relieved you of

	your anxieties, and none of this need have happened.
CHEVALIER:	You won't find me making advances to you: I don't even dream of that with you.
MARQUISE:	I absolutely forbid it, that is not in the terms of our agreement, I could also be jealous myself, but jealous as we understand it.
CHEVALIER:	You, Madame?
MARQUISE:	Wasn't I a little like that earlier; your response to Lisette, didn't that upset me?
CHEVALIER:	You did say some very cruel things to me.
MARQUISE:	Eh! who else can we say them to, if not to those we most care about and who appear unresponsive?
CHEVALIER:	Dare I believe you? You're making me feel so tranquil, my dear Marquise!
MARQUISE:	Believe me, I had as much need of this clarification as you.
CHEVALIER:	You charm away my cares! You fill me with joy! *(He kisses her hand.)*
MARQUISE:	*(Laughing.)* You'd take him for my lover, from the way he thanks me.
CHEVALIER:	I swear, I defy any lover to love you more than I do, I'd never have believed that friendship could touch such depths, it's overwhelming, more alive than love.
MARQUISE:	Yet it never reaches too far.
CHEVALIER:	No, never too far, but there is just one favour to ask of you. Do you intend to retain Hortensius? I think he dislikes seeing me around, and I can read every bit as well as he does.
MARQUISE:	Then, Chevalier, we'll have to send him away, that's all we need do.
CHEVALIER:	And the Count, what shall we do with him? He does disturb me somewhat.

MARQUISE: We'll send him away, too. I wish only for you to be happy, I wish to bring you some peace; give me your hand, I'd like very much to stroll in the garden.

CHEVALIER: Let's go, Marquise.

End of Act Two.

ACT THREE

SCENE 1

HORTENSIUS alone

HORTENSIUS: Strange, is it not, that a man such as myself, is totally without means? To possess Latin and Greek but not a silver piece to my name! Oh, sacred Homer! Divine Virgil! And you charming Anacreon, your learnèd interpreter barely makes ends meet; I'll shortly be thown in the gutter; one moment, I see the Marquise quarrelling with the Chevalier; the next, there she is, in the garden, chattering with him in the most familiar fashion. What inappropriate conduct! Is it love that's going to drive me out of this household?

SCENE 2

HORTENSIUS, LISETTE, LUBIN

LUBIN: That's handy, Lisette, look, he's here, we can bid him goodbye. *(Laughing.)* Ah, ah, ah!

HORTENSIUS: What's sent this oaf into such transports of joy?

LUBIN: Come on, give us a smile, comrade Doctor, how goes philosophy?

HORTENSIUS: What sort of question is that?

LUBIN: Good grief, I've no idea, if it isn't a conversation opener.

LISETTE: Come on, come on, let's get this dealt with.

LUBIN: Just one brief word, Doctor, have you ever slept in the street?

HORTENSIUS: What is the significance of this conversation?

LUBIN:	It's just that tonight you're going to have that pleasure: the north wind will have a couple of words to whisper in your ear.
LISETTE:	No more fooling with the doctor: here, Monsieur, Madame has asked me to give you this gold, in return for which, since she's taking leave of you, you may take leave of her. On my own account, I bow to your learning, and remain your very humble servant. *(She curtsies.)*
LUBIN:	A little bow from me, too.
HORTENSIUS:	What, Madame's dismissing me?
LISETTE:	Not at all, Monsieur, she simply asks you to withdraw your services.
LUBIN:	And being the decent man you are, you won't refuse her.
HORTENSIUS:	Do you know the reason for this, Mad'moiselle Lisette?
LISETTE:	No: but roughly I suspect she might be finding you tiresome.
LUBIN:	And, more to the point, we'll feel more at ease doing our loving without all that head-bound philosophy of yours telling us not to.
LISETTE:	Be quiet.
HORTENSIUS:	I understand why: it's because Madame the Marquise and Monsieur the Chevalier are inclined to one another.
LISETTE:	I know nothing about that, it's none of my business.
LUBIN:	Well, every cloud has a silver lining; when there's inclination, when there's passion, sighs, flames and a wedding to follow, then there's nothing so joyous; people have hearts and they make use of them, what could be more natural.
LISETTE:	*(To LUBIN.)* Enough of your nonsense. *(To HORTENSIUS.)* You've been notified,

	Monsieur, I don't think we need say anything more.
LUBIN:	So long then, put it there and part smartly; it wouldn't hurt to step off at the double.
HORTENSIUS:	Tell Madame I shall conform to her behest.

SCENE 3

LISETTE, LUBIN

LISETTE:	At last, that's him sent packing, all the same that's one lover the less.
LUBIN:	Lover! What, that old driveller was in love with you?
LISETTE:	Certainly; he wanted to make syllogisms with me.
LUBIN:	Hum!
LISETTE:	Syllogisms, but let me tell you, I repelled his advances with some of my own.
LUBIN:	Syllogisms! Why don't you repel my advances with one so I can see what they're like.
LISETTE:	Nothing easier. Ready? Here we go: You're a nice-looking lad.
LUBIN:	True.
LISETTE:	I love everything that looks nice, therefore I love you: that's what you call a syllogism.
LUBIN:	Hold on, you don't need to be a philosopher for that. I can make one just as good. Let's wager a little kiss that I can come up with a dozen for you.
LISETTE:	I'll take that bet when we're married, then I'll be more than happy to lose.
LUBIN:	Fine! And when we're married, I won't need a bet in order to win.
LISETTE:	Shush, I can hear someone, Monsieur the Count, I think; Madame has a message for him that won't exactly thrill him.

SCENE 4

COUNT, LISETTE, LUBIN

COUNT: *(Looking shaken.)* Lisette, I've just seen Hortensius, he's been telling me some very strange things: the Marquise has dismissed him, because, according to him, she is in love with the Chevalier and is preparing to marry him. Is this true? I beg you to throw some light on this.

LISETTE: But, Monsieur the Count, I don't think that can be so, I've seen no indications of it: she was dissatisfied with Hortensius, so she let him go; that's all I can tell you.

COUNT: *(To LUBIN.)* And you, can you add anything to this?

LUBIN: No, Monsieur the Count, I can only tell you about my love for Lisette; that's all I know.

LISETTE: Madame the Marquise is so little inclined to marry, she doesn't even wish to receive admirers; in fact I'm to beg you not to persist in paying court to her.

COUNT: And never to see her again, I presume.

LISETTE: I think it amounts to the same thing.

LUBIN: Yes, if you say one thing, you say the other.

COUNT: Women are utterly unpredictable! The Chevalier is around, I gather?

LISETTE: I believe so.

LUBIN: Their feelings of friendship prevent them from keeping apart.

COUNT: Ah! inform the Chevalier, if you would, that I'd like a word with him.

LISETTE: I'm on my way, Monsieur the Count. *(She and LUBIN bow and leave.)*

SCENE 5

COUNT, alone

COUNT: What's the meaning of this? Do they love one another? When the Chevalier gets here, I'll probe his feelings and draw out the truth. I'll make use of a very common strategy, common but rarely known to fail.

SCENE 6

CHEVALIER, COUNT

CHEVALIER: You wish to see me; can I be of service, Monsieur?

COUNT: Yes, Chevalier, you certainly can.

CHEVALIER: Then, consider yourself served.

COUNT: You told me you did not love the Marquise.

CHEVALIER: What do you mean? I love her with all my heart.

COUNT: I was given to understand that you weren't the least in love with her.

CHEVALIER: Ah! that's a completely different matter on which I've made myself clear.

COUNT: I know that, but are your feelings still the same? Haven't they now become feelings of real love?

CHEVALIER: *(Laughs.)* Eh! but, really, how do you judge that to be the case? What sort of suggestion is that?

COUNT: Myself, I'm not judging, I'm asking.

CHEVALIER: Hum! Nonetheless you do have the expression of a man who's already made up his mind.

COUNT: Well, disencumber yourself of that idea, tell me, yes or no.

CHEVALIER: *(Laughing.)* Eh, eh, Monsieur the Count, a man of the world such as yourself shouldn't quibble over words; 'yes' or 'no' never occurred to me, they aren't any clearer than the words I used; they mean absolutely the same: the Marquise and I share a friendship based on wholly honourable feelings: does that satisfy you? Is that clear? it is French.

COUNT: *(Aside.)* Not entirely...I couldn't have put it more clearly myself, and I was in the wrong, but you have to forgive lovers, they're suspicious of everything.

CHEVALIER: I know that only too well from myself. But to return to the state of your heart, I very much take an interest in your concerns: but don't distort what I'm about to say to you; open your heart to me. Are you resolved to go on loving the Marquise?

COUNT: For ever.

CHEVALIER: *Entre nous,* I'm astonished you haven't grown tired of her indifference. For heaven's sake, a woman has to express some feeling: she hates you? You can combat the hatred; she doesn't dislike you? There's room for hope; but a woman who is completely unresponsive, how do you deal with her? How can you capture her heart? A heart that doesn't move one way or another, that's neither friend nor enemy, that's empty, dead, can you bring such a heart back to life? I don't think you can: but that's what you're determined to do.

COUNT: *(Smoothly.)* No, no, Chevalier, it's my turn to talk to you in confidence. I'm not reduced to pursuing a totally phantom endeavour: the heart of the Marquise is not as dead as you think. Did you hear what I just said? You seem distracted.

CHEVALIER: You're mistaken, I've never been more attentive.

COUNT: She's aware of my love, I've spoken of it and she listened.

CHEVALIER:	She listened.
COUNT:	Yes, I asked for her response.
CHEVALIER:	That is the custom; how did she reply?
COUNT:	She asked me to give her time.
CHEVALIER:	Well, that's clear enough.
COUNT:	*(Aside.)* He loves her… However, today she refuses to see me, I attribute that to my negligence: I failed to call on her for a few days prior to your return; the Marquise is the proudest woman in France.
CHEVALIER:	She'd be justified in her pride, if she felt taken for granted.
COUNT:	I asked you earlier to intercede with her on my behalf, and I'm asking you again.
CHEVALIER:	Come, you're making fun of me, this woman adores you!
COUNT:	I don't quite say that.
CHEVALIER:	It's hardly my concern, but I'm saying it for you.
COUNT:	It's gratifying that you say it without jealousy.
CHEVALIER:	Oh! Good heavens! If that gratifies you, I can go on gratifying you to your heart's content: let me tell you how delighted I am for you, how warmly I congratulate you, how happily I embrace you.
COUNT:	Then embrace me, my dear friend.
CHEVALIER:	Ah! unnecessary, it's more than enough to rejoice for you; sincerely; and I'll give you completely unambiguous proof of that.
COUNT:	I'd very much like to show you my gratitude, I really would, and if you were in the right mood to accept what I'm considering, I'd be totally certain about you. With respect to the Marquise…
CHEVALIER:	Count, let's move on: you lovers can think of nothing but love, only love and what concerns love; all that madness isn't quite so

absorbing for the rest of us; let's change the
subject, what were you about to propose?

COUNT: Tell me, my dear friend, have you definitely
given up all idea of marriage?

CHEVALIER: Oh, dear heaven! This is taking matters far
too far: do I have to renounce marriage to
put your mind, once and for all, at rest? No,
Monsieur, I beg you to consider my posterity
– if you'd be so good. I shan't poach on your
preserves, but let someone find me a suitable
partner and I'll marry tomorrow: and I'll go
further, the Marquise, whom you can't get out
of your mind, well, I promise to invite her to
the ceremony.

COUNT: Upon my soul, Chevalier, you overwhelm
me, I feel I'm dealing with the most open-
hearted, the most open-handed of men; your
attitude soothes all my concerns. My dear
friend, let's pursue what I started to say:
you're familiar with my sister; what do you
think of her?

CHEVALIER: What do I think?… Your question reminds
me it's a long while since I've been in her
company, you'll have to present me to her
again.

COUNT: You've told me a hundred times that she
deserved the love of a truly honourable man;
she's highly thought of, you know her as a
woman of considerable means. She would
like you, of that I'm certain, so if you're
looking for a suitable partner, here she is.

CHEVALIER: Here she is…you're right…yes…your
suggestion is admirable; she's a friend of the
Marquise, is she not?

COUNT: I believe so.

CHEVALIER: Very well, it's done, but I'd like to be the one
to announce the matter; I think she's coming,
withdraw into this study for a few moments;

you'll see what a rival of my sort can do, and you'll appear when I call you; go, now, no expressions of gratitude, jealous rivals don't deserve any.

SCENE 7

CHEVALIER alone

CHEVALIER: Dear God, Madame, I'm supposed to be this friend who comes before all others; you've been toying with me like any other woman, but I'll show you how little I care.

SCENE 8

MARQUISE, CHEVALIER

MARQUISE: Did I hear the Count was with you, Chevalier? And for quite a while, what was that about?

CHEVALIER: *(Gravely.)* Pure fantasies on his part, Marquise, but fantasies that offend me, because they involve you, and the first and foremost was to enquire whether I loved you.

MARQUISE: But I thought that wasn't in question.

CHEVALIER: Not in question at all: but best beware, he was speaking of love, not friendship.

MARQUISE: Ah! he spoke of love? He's very inquisitive: had it been me, I wouldn't have bothered to make the distinction, let him work it out for himself.

CHEVALIER: Not possible, Madame, there was no room to manoeuvre, he had enveloped you in suspicions, and endowed your heart with more tenderness for me than I deserve. You can see how serious he was, I was forced to give him a clear-cut answer, so I did: I assured him that he was misguided, and that there was absolutely no love between us, absolutely none.

MARQUISE: But d'you think you convinced him, d'you think you told him in a persuasive tone of voice, the tone of a man who believes what he says?

CHEVALIER: Oh! never fear: I spoke with utter sincerity; how else! I'd be extremely angry on your behalf if the conduct of our friendship exposed your feelings to any ambiguous interpretations, my attachment to you is far too delicate to exploit the honour it bestows on me; but I've put everything back in good order – and by one of those unforeseen events: you know his sister, rich, charming, one of your friends even.

MARQUISE: Slightly.

CHEVALIER: In his joy at having his suspicions laid to rest, the Count offered me her hand in marriage; there are those sudden moments in life, those unexpected thoughts, that all at once determine your future, I played my designated role; we came to an agreement and I'm to marry her. That's not all, I'm once again charged to speak to you in the Count's favour; and I do so in the most positive way possible; your heart isn't unyielding, and I don't believe the proposition inappropriate.

MARQUISE: *(Coldly.)* No, Monsieur, I admit that the Count has never displeased me.

CHEVALIER: Never displeased you! That's good to know. So why did you tell me to the contrary?

MARQUISE: I was trying to hide what I felt from myself – and from the Count, who knew nothing of it.

CHEVALIER: No longer, Madame, he's been listening to you.

MARQUISE: He has?

SCENE 9

COUNT, MARQUISE, CHEVALIER

COUNT: I've followed the Chevalier's advice,
Madame; allow my rapture to convey to you
the joy I feel. *(He throws himself on his knees at
her feet.)*

MARQUISE: Get up, Count, you may hope.

COUNT: I'm in ecstasy! And you, Chevalier, dear
friend, what don't I owe to you? But,
Madame, complete my destiny as the
most fulfilled of men. Chevalier, join your
entreaties to mine.

CHEVALIER: *(Agitated.)* You have no need of them,
Monsieur, I promised to speak for you, I've
kept my word, now I shall leave you together
and withdraw. *(Aside.)* I'm dying.

COUNT: I'll find you at your place.

SCENE 10

MARQUISE, COUNT

COUNT: Madame, my heart has been yours for a long
while, agree to my happiness, let this occasion
decide for you: often it needs no more than
that. I have some business at my notary's
this evening, I could fetch him here, we
could take supper with my sister, she should
be calling on you: the Chevalier will be
there; you can decide what you'd like to do;
contracts are easily dealt with; they can be
drawn up as soon as you say the word: don't
refuse me, I implore you.

MARQUISE: I'm not able to reply just now, I feel a little
unwell; allow me, if you would: I need to rest.

COUNT: I'll continue with the arrangements in the
hope that they'll encourage you to indulge
me.

SCENE 11

MARQUISE alone

MARQUISE: I don't know where I am; let me breathe, where are these sighs coming from? tears flowing; I feel overwhelmed by so much sadness, and I don't know why. Is it my friendship with the Chevalier? That ingrate's getting married: a lover's unfaithfulness would barely touch me, but a friend's – it plunges me into despair. The Count's in love with me, I've said I don't dislike him, true; but what have I done to bring all this on myself?

SCENE 12

LISETTE, MARQUISE

LISETTE: Madame, I'm just letting you know the Count's sister's been told you're not receiving calls, she said she'd pass by this evening; does that suit you?

MARQUISE: No, never, Lisette; on no account.

LISETTE: Aren't you well. Madame? you look utterly dejected, what on earth's the matter?

MARQUISE: Alas, Lisette, they're persecuting me, I'm expected to marry.

LISETTE: Marry! Who?

MARQUISE: The most loathsome of men, a man misfortune has destined to make me unhappy, who's snatched words out of my mouth in spite of myself, without my knowing what I was saying.

LISETTE: But the Count's the only one who's been here.

MARQUISE: Eh! That's who it is.

LISETTE: And you're marrying him?

MARQUISE: I don't know anything anymore; he claims so.

LISETTE:	He claims so? What is going on? It doesn't make sense.
MARQUISE:	I don't now how to make it clearer to you; it's the Chevalier, it's that miserable man who's to blame for all this: he got me upset, the Count took advantage of it, don't ask me how; they're coming to take supper here this evening; they're talking of a notary, contracts; I just let them talk; the Chevalier's gone, he's also getting married; the Count has promised his sister's hand to him; that's all I needed, a sister to complete my misery, as to that man…
LISETTE:	What do you care if the Chevalier marries?
MARQUISE:	Do you want me to be the sister-in-law of a man who's become unbearable to me?
LISETTE:	Ha! give me strength, you don't have to be, send the Count packing.
MARQUISE:	Ha! on what pretext? He does aggravate me, but, even so, I've nothing to reproach him with.
LISETTE:	Oh! you've lost me, Madame; I don't understand a thing.
MARQUISE:	Nor I: I don't know where I am, I don't know how to extricate myself, I'm dying! what sort of state am I in?
LISETTE:	I'm convinced that cursèd Chevalier is the cause of all this; and personally I'm convinced he's in love with you.
MARQUISE:	Eh! no, Lisette, anyone can see you're mistaken.
LISETTE:	Why won't you believe me, Madame, don't ever see him again.
MARQUISE:	Eh! leave me alone, Lisette, you're persecuting me just like the rest of them! Am I never to be left in peace? Truly, truly, my situation is nothing short of tragic.

LISETTE: Your situation; I see it more as an enigma.

SCENE 13

LUBIN, LISETTE, MARQUISE

LUBIN: Madame, Monsieur the Chevalier, who's in such a state, you could weep...

MARQUISE: What's he talking about? Find out what he wants, Lisette.

LUBIN: Alas! I think he's losing his reason: sometimes he's pacing, sometimes he just comes to a standstill; he stares at the sky as if he'd never seen it before: he says one thing, he stammers another, and he's sent me to find out if you'd be willing to see him.

MARQUISE: You don't advise me to see him, do you, that's right, isn't it, yes?

LISETTE: Yes, Madame, from the way you ask that question, that's what I advise.

LUBIN: First off, he wrote a letter for me to give you.

MARQUISE: Let me see it.

LUBIN: This instant, Madame; when I took the letter, he ran after me: Give it back, I give it back; Here, go and deliver it, so I take it again; Bring it back, I take it back; the next thing, he drops it while he's pacing about, and I picked it up without him seeing, so I could bring it to you as his good friend, to see if there's any cure for his sufferings in it.

MARQUISE: Show me.

LUBIN: Here it is: and here's the writer.

SCENE 14

CHEVALIER, MARQUISE, LUBIN, LISETTE

MARQUISE: *(To LISETTE.)* Leave us, it's probably easier without witnesses, on our own.

SCENE 15

CHEVALIER, MARQUISE

CHEVALIER: *(Entering slowly by a roundabout route.)* I've come to take my leave and bid you adieu, Madame.

MARQUISE: You, Monsieur the Chevalier, and where are you off to?

CHEVALIER: Where I was going before you urged me to stay.

MARQUISE: I didn't intend your stay to be so brief.

CHEVALIER: Nor I to leave so soon, definitely not.

MARQUISE: Then why are you leaving me?

CHEVALIER: Why am I leaving you? Eh! Marquise, what will my absence matter to you, now that you're marrying the Count!

MARQUISE: Wait, Chevalier, and you'll see there's still a misunderstanding between us; don't do anything rash, I don't want you to go, I'd rather be the one in the wrong.

CHEVALIER: No, Marquise, it's done: I can't stay, my heart would no longer be in harmony with yours.

MARQUISE: *(Sadly.)* I think you're making a mistake.

CHEVALIER: If only you knew how sincerely I'm speaking, how incompatible our feelings are…

MARQUISE: Why incompatible? What you're saying, Chevalier, needs a little more explanation, I really don't understand.

CHEVALIER: There's only one word stopping me.

MARQUISE: *(With some discomfort.)* I can't guess it, if you won't tell me.

CHEVALIER: A while ago I explained in a letter to you.

MARQUISE: Oh, yes, a letter was handed to me just as you arrived.

CHEVALIER: *(Perplexed.)* From whom, Madame?

MARQUISE: I'll tell you. *(She reads.)* 'I thought, Madame, that I'd regret the loss of Angélique all my life; however, will you believe this? I'm leaving filled with as much love for you as I ever felt for her.'

CHEVALIER: Will what you've read, Madame, affect me?

MARQUISE: Wait, Chevalier, isn't that the word that stopped you?

CHEVALIER: It is my letter! Ah! Marquise, tell me, what is my future to be?

MARQUISE: I'm blushing, Chevalier, that's for you to say?

CHEVALIER: *(Kissing her hand.)* My love for you will last as long as my life.

MARQUISE: Only on that condition do I forgive you.

SCENE 16

MARQUISE, CHEVALIER, COUNT

COUNT: What's this? Monsieur the Chevalier in raptures?

CHEVALIER: It's true, Monsieur the Count, when you accused me of loving Madame, you knew my heart better than I did; but it's what I truly believed then, and I'm sure you'll find this excusable.

COUNT: And you, Madame?

MARQUISE: I'd never have thought friendship could be so dangerous.

COUNT: Ah, heavens!

SCENE 17

LISETTE, LUBIN, MARQUISE, CHEVALIER

LISETTE: Madame, there's a notary outside, he came with the Count.

CHEVALIER: Shall we retain his services, Madame?

MARQUISE: You decide, I'm not getting involved in anything more.

LISETTE: *(To the CHEVALIER.)* Ah! I'm beginning to get the picture: the Count's going, the notary's staying, and you're marrying.

LUBIN: Us, too; your contract will be the basis of ours: right, Lisette? What happiness!

THE END.